Jesus from A to Z

By Kevin W. Graham
Illustrated by Jennifer H. Yoswa

Windom Publishing Company
Denver, Colorado

Published by Windom Publishing Company

Windom Publishing Company
PO Box 102225
Denver, CO 80250
windompublishing@yahoo.com
www.jesusfromatoz.com

Library of Congress Cataloging-in-Publication Data

Graham, Kevin, 1959-
Jesus from A to Z / by Kevin W. Graham; illustrated by Jennifer H. Yoswa, illustrator.
p. cm.
1. Jesus Christ – Biography – Juvenile literature. 2. Bible stories, English – N.T. – Juvenile literature.
3. Christianity – Juvenile literature. 4. Alphabet books. I. Yoswa, Jennifer H., 1963- II. Title. 232.901 – 22.
Library of Congress Control Number: 2008932741
ISBN: 978-0-9700323-1-7

This book is available at special discounts when purchased in bulk quantities for churches, associations, institutions or promotions. Please contact Windom Publishing Co. at windompublishing@yahoo.com.

Website Address: www.jesusfromatoz.com

Printed in China

Design by studio sb

10 9 8 7 6 5 4 3 2 1

For my sons, Aaron and Lex, my brightest lights
–K.G.

For my mom, Faith, who inspired this artistic journey
–J.Y.

Acknowledgements
Special thanks to Jim Dudley, who suggested the concept behind this book as a way to introduce his children to the stories of Jesus' life, along with the alphabet. We also send thanks to the many friends, family members, and literary professionals who have helped bring this book to life.

The following pages hold short and concise versions of the stories of Jesus' life. They are designed to allow adults to introduce young readers to the alphabet and life of Jesus in a child-friendly manner. Older readers may wish to expand on these stories, adding details and sharing the stories' larger meaning with the young people in their lives.

A ANGELS – Angels are God's helpers who appear at special times. An angel named Gabriel came to tell Mary that she would have a baby and become the mother of Jesus. Other angels told the shepherds to go to the town of Bethlehem to see Jesus the night he was born. Angels appeared at different times in Jesus' life. They helped bring God's word to everyone.

B BOAT – Jesus fell asleep during a boat ride with his good friends, the disciples. He took a nap after a long day of talking with people. Suddenly, a terrible storm came up. Waves crashed into the boat. The disciples were frightened. They shook Jesus awake, and he could see how scared they were. Jesus stood up and told the storm to stop. And it did! He taught the disciples to believe in the power of God.

C CHILDREN – Lots of people brought their children with them to see Jesus. The children liked to sit with Jesus and listen to him. At first, Jesus' disciples didn't think the children should be there. The disciples thought the children would bother Jesus. But Jesus welcomed the boys and girls. He said, "Let the children come to me because the Kingdom of God belongs to them." Jesus said that heaven is for anyone who is open and trusting, like a child.

D DONKEY – Jesus came back to the city of Jerusalem on a day we now call Palm Sunday. He rode into the city on the back of a small donkey, not in a fancy chariot. Riding a donkey was a humble way for Jesus to return. It showed he came in peace. Many people came and laid palm branches on the road in front of Jesus to welcome him. They loved Jesus and his stories.

E

EMPTY TOMB – Three days after Jesus died, two of Jesus' friends discovered that his tomb was empty. They were very sad. They thought someone had taken his body. Jesus' friends didn't know that he had come back to life after dying on a cross. An angel then greeted the two women and told them the good news – that Jesus had come back to life. He had overcome death. This is the reason we celebrate Easter.

FISH – Jesus spoke to a crowd of five thousand people one afternoon. Afterward, he knew the people were hungry. But there were only two fish and five loaves of bread. Jesus took this small amount of food and asked God to help him. The amount of food grew and grew when Jesus started passing it out. Everyone had plenty of bread and fish. Feeding this group of five thousand people is one of Jesus' greatest miracles.

GOOD SAMARITAN – One of Jesus' best stories is about a man from Samaria called the Good Samaritan. Robbers attacked a traveler and left him to die by the side of a road. Two men came across the injured man, but they walked by and didn't help him. Then the Good Samaritan came along. Although people in the area didn't like people from Samaria, this Samaritan decided to help the man. In telling this story, Jesus showed that a neighbor is anyone from anywhere who needs your help.

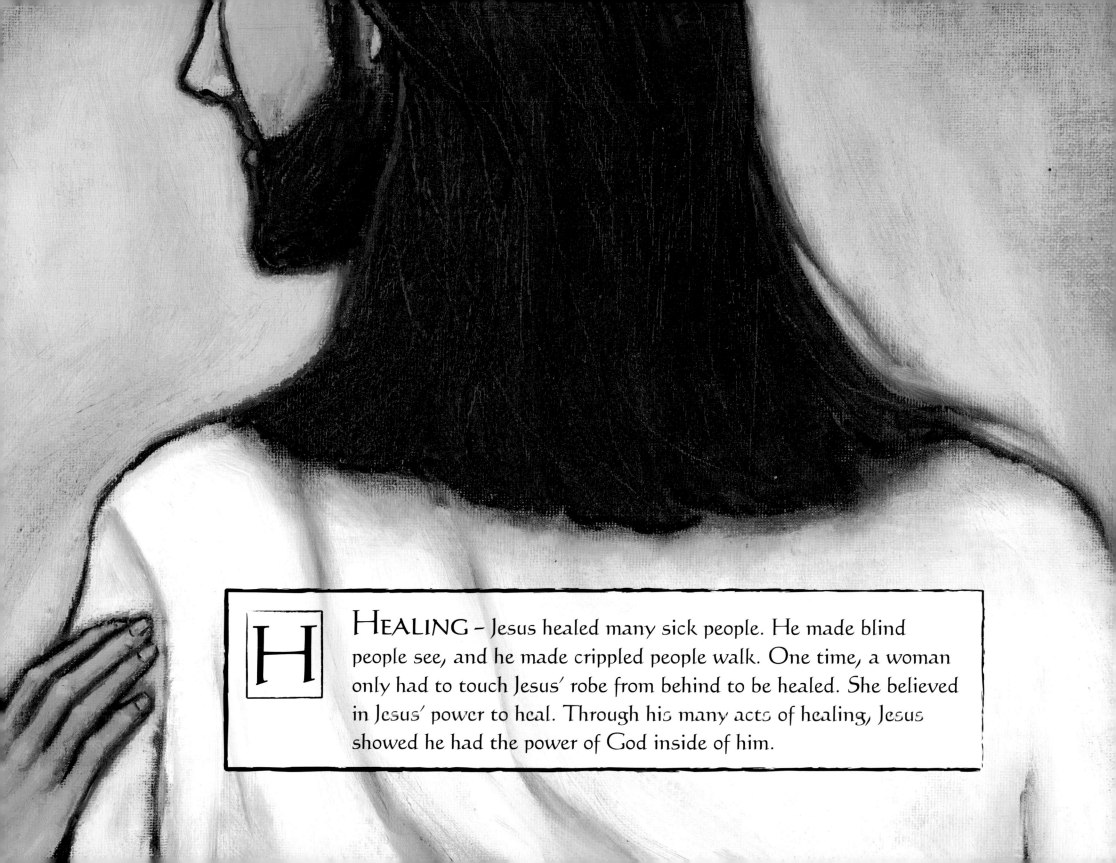

HEALING – Jesus healed many sick people. He made blind people see, and he made crippled people walk. One time, a woman only had to touch Jesus' robe from behind to be healed. She believed in Jesus' power to heal. Through his many acts of healing, Jesus showed he had the power of God inside of him.

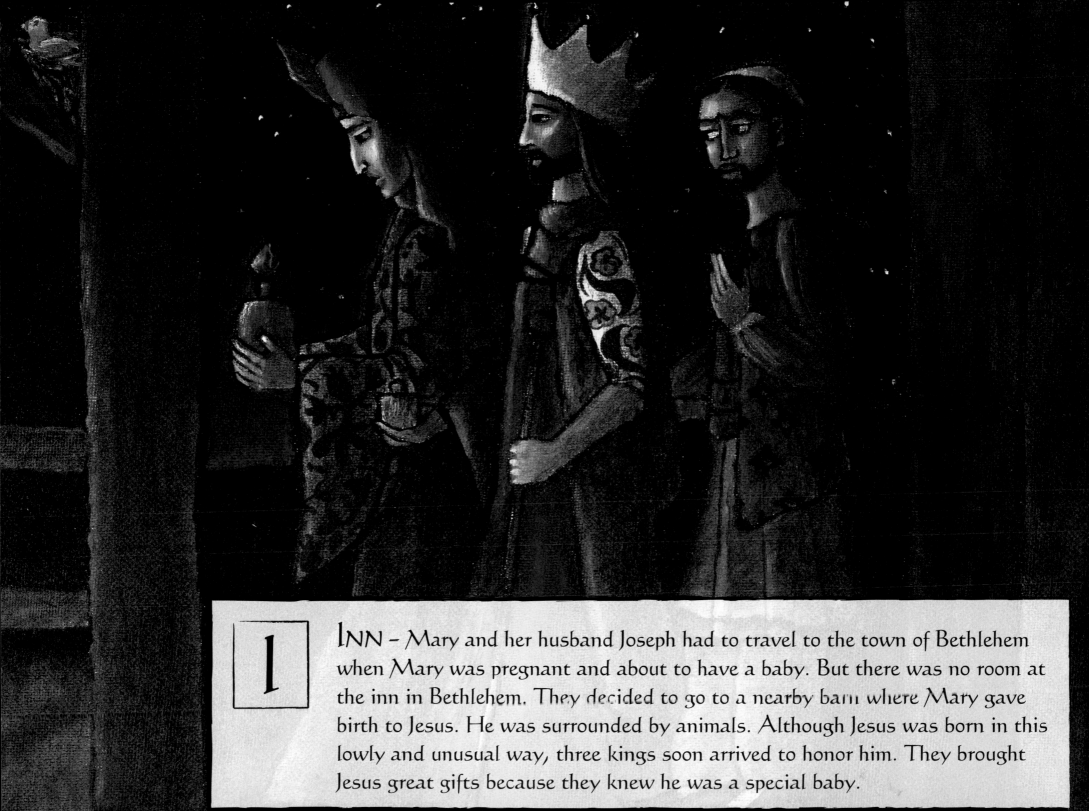

1 INN – Mary and her husband Joseph had to travel to the town of Bethlehem when Mary was pregnant and about to have a baby. But there was no room at the inn in Bethlehem. They decided to go to a nearby barn where Mary gave birth to Jesus. He was surrounded by animals. Although Jesus was born in this lowly and unusual way, three kings soon arrived to honor him. They brought Jesus great gifts because they knew he was a special baby.

J JOHN THE BAPTIST – John the Baptist was Jesus' cousin. People came from far away to hear John speak, just as they would travel a long way to hear Jesus speak. One day, Jesus came to see John at the Jordan River. John lowered Jesus into the river, giving Jesus a special blessing called baptism. Afterward, a dove landed on Jesus' shoulder. This was a sign that God was present at Jesus' baptism.

KINGDOM OF GOD – Jesus said the Kingdom of God is inside every one of us. It also is found wherever people love and serve God. Jesus taught his disciples about God's kingdom, which he also sometimes called the Kingdom of Heaven. Jesus taught many people the Lord's Prayer. In it, we speak of the Kingdom of God. The prayer says of God, "Thy kingdom come, thy will be done, on Earth as it is in Heaven."

LAZARUS – Friends of Jesus knew their brother Lazarus was sick. They asked Jesus to come right away to help, but he couldn't. Lazarus had been dead for four days when Jesus finally arrived. Still, Jesus went to the tomb where Lazarus was buried. In front of a crowd of people, Jesus called to Lazarus and asked him to come out of the tomb. Lazarus walked out, still wrapped in clothing from his grave. Bringing Lazarus back from death is one of Jesus' many miracles.

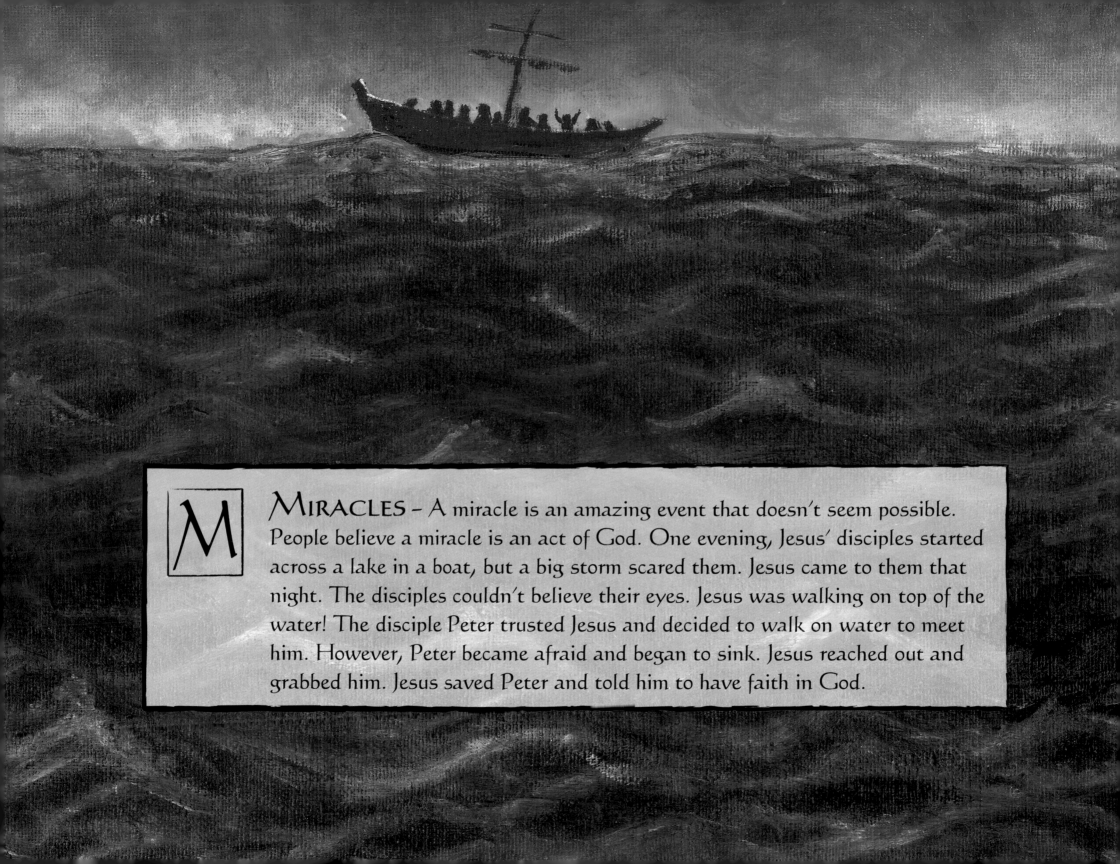

MIRACLES – A miracle is an amazing event that doesn't seem possible. People believe a miracle is an act of God. One evening, Jesus' disciples started across a lake in a boat, but a big storm scared them. Jesus came to them that night. The disciples couldn't believe their eyes. Jesus was walking on top of the water! The disciple Peter trusted Jesus and decided to walk on water to meet him. However, Peter became afraid and began to sink. Jesus reached out and grabbed him. Jesus saved Peter and told him to have faith in God.

NEW TESTAMENT – The New Testament is the part of the Bible that tells of Jesus' life and his teachings. It also tells what happened after Jesus came back to life to show God's love for everyone. The first four chapters of the New Testament are the Gospels. They are called Matthew, Mark, Luke, and John. In them, four different people tell the stories of Jesus and his life on Earth.

O **OLIVE** – Olive trees and the oil made from their fruit were an important part of everyday life in Jesus' time. Olive oil was used to make food, to light lamps, for cleaning, and for special ceremonies. Olive trees can live for a very long time. One of Jesus' favorite places to pray to God was on the Mount of Olives near Jerusalem, where olive trees still grow today.

PRODIGAL SON – Prodigal means wasteful. Jesus told the story of the Prodigal Son, who left his home and wasted a lot of money. When the Prodigal Son returned home, he was very sad and troubled by what he had done. He hoped only to work as a servant for his father. His brother, who stayed home and worked hard, was mad. But the boys' father was very happy and threw a big party. He was glad his Prodigal Son had come home. By telling this story – of a father forgiving his son's mistakes – Jesus showed that God's forgiveness is for everyone.

Q QUIET – Most kids know about quiet time. It is a time to calm down, rest, and be still. This quiet time can happen after someone gets in trouble. Or it can happen after a fun time of running around and laughing. Quiet time also can be a time to think of God and Jesus, and be thankful for everything we have here on Earth. It can be a time to quietly remember the fun of running and laughing, and to know that having fun is a gift from God.

ROOF – A man who was sick and could not walk had some very good friends. They carried him to Jesus to be healed. But they couldn't get close because of the crowd of people gathered around to listen to Jesus. So his friends carried their friend up to the roof, made a hole in it, and lowered him down on a small bed. Jesus said to their friend, "Pick up your bed and walk," and he did. Everyone was amazed and happy that Jesus performed this miracle, once again showing his connection to God.

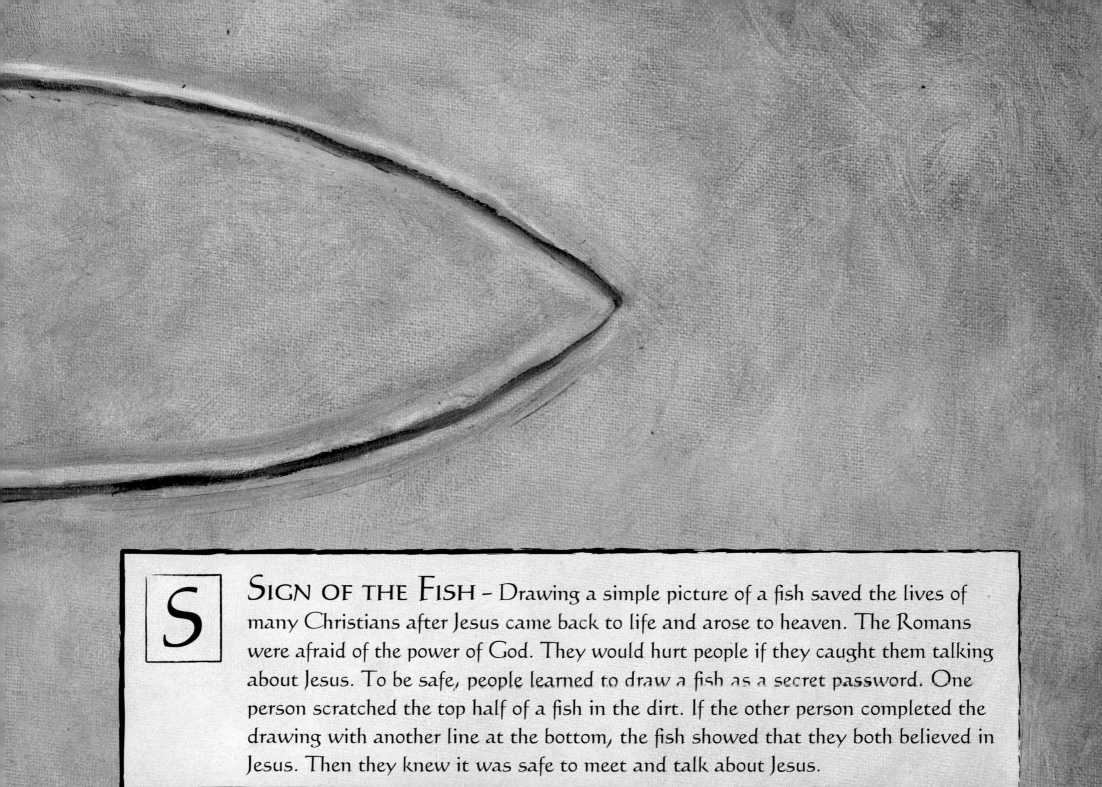

SIGN OF THE FISH – Drawing a simple picture of a fish saved the lives of many Christians after Jesus came back to life and arose to heaven. The Romans were afraid of the power of God. They would hurt people if they caught them talking about Jesus. To be safe, people learned to draw a fish as a secret password. One person scratched the top half of a fish in the dirt. If the other person completed the drawing with another line at the bottom, the fish showed that they both believed in Jesus. Then they knew it was safe to meet and talk about Jesus.

TWELVE DISCIPLES – Jesus asked twelve people to be his helpers. They were called the disciples. Although they were just regular men, they also were his students who learned from Jesus and followed him. Some of them were fishermen. Jesus told them he would teach them to "fish for men." Jesus meant that he would teach the disciples to spread the news of God's love for mankind.

U UPPER ROOM – The night before Jesus died, he shared a special meal with his disciples in the upper room of a house. We remember this meal and call it the Last Supper. Jesus washed the feet of his disciples as if he was a servant to show that no person is greater than another. He also served bread and wine to the disciples. He told them that the bread was his body and the wine was his blood – signs of God's love. He asked them to remember him. The disciples knew something would happen to Jesus soon.

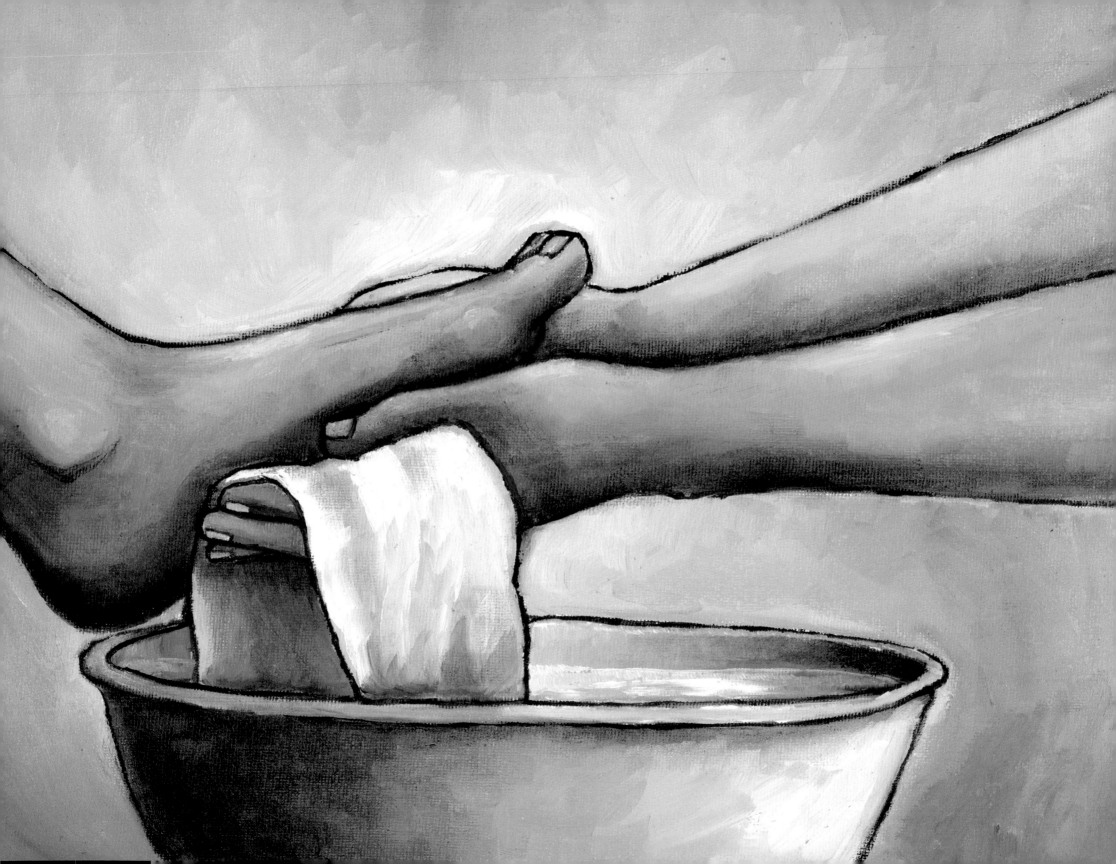

V VIA DOLOROSA – Three days before Easter, Jesus was forced to carry a wooden cross up a long street on his way to die on the cross. This street in Jerusalem is now known as the "way of sadness," or Via Dolorosa in the Latin language. Today, many people come to walk the same street. It helps them remember that Jesus died and then came back to life to show God's love for everyone.

WEDDING AT CANA – Jesus enjoyed parties like the rest of us. He once went to a wedding party with his disciples and his mother, Mary. During the party, the wine ran out. Mary knew the power inside Jesus and asked him to help. Jesus decided to perform his first miracle. He asked the servants to fill several large jars with water. When the water was served to the guests, it had turned into wine! In doing this, Jesus first showed the power of God inside him. He also showed that he, too, was a person filled with the joy of life.

eXPLAIN – One of Jesus' favorite ways to explain things was to use parables. Parables are stories, like the story of the Good Samaritan, which teach us about life. Jesus was a great storyteller. He used parables to say many important things. Some people call Jesus' parables stories about life on Earth, but with meanings that involve Heaven. In one of his parables, Jesus told a story about a shepherd who left his flock of sheep to go find just one that was lost. In this parable, Jesus said that God, like a shepherd, also cares for every one of us.

YAHWEH – There are many names for God. Some are fun to say, like "Yahweh," while others are short and simple like "Lord." Jesus showed people that there is a God, and that God loves the Earth and everything on it – no matter what name he is called. All of Jesus' miracles and stories told people about the greatness of God, who Jesus said is like a loving parent.

Z ZACCHEUS - A man named Zaccheus collected money from people as a tax collector. But sometimes Zaccheus cheated people and took extra money from them. When he heard that Jesus was coming, Zaccheus climbed a tree to get a better view of Jesus. Jesus knew that Zaccheus had stolen money. He asked Zaccheus to come down and visit with him. After meeting Jesus, Zaccheus said he was sorry and returned the money he had stolen. He also gave money to poor people who didn't have as much money as he did. Zaccheus saw that other things were more important than money. Jesus helped Zaccheus change his life.